MARTIN

BIG

THE LIFE OF DR. MAR

'S

WORDS

TIN LUTHER KING, JR.

DOREEN RAPPAPORT

ILLUSTRATED BY BRYAN COLLIER

JUMP AT THE SUN HYPERION PAPERBACKS FOR CHILDREN/*New York*

Printed in Singapore
This book is set in Fenice.
The art was prepared using watercolor and cut paper collage.

First Jump at the Sun paperback edition, 2007
7 9 10 8 6
F850-6835-5-10341

Library of Congress Cataloging-in-Publication Data on file.

ISBN-13: 978-14231-0635-7
ISBN-10: 1-4231-0635-0

Visit www.jumpatthesun.com

To Isaac with love, from Grandma Dorzi.—D.R.

To Joe, the custodian at Washington High School,
who encouraged me to always dream. Thank you.—B.C.

AUTHOR'S NOTE

I was introduced to the philosophy of nonviolence as a high school student in 1955 during the Montgomery bus boycott and as a teacher during the Southern sit-ins of the 1960s. The courage and determination of the Southern black Americans who confronted violence with nonviolence transformed my life and ideas. I went to the March on Washington in 1963 to support this inspirational movement. I went South to teach in a Mississippi freedom school during the summer of 1965. In Mississippi I saw firsthand the fragility of being black in white America.

Dr. Martin Luther King, Jr., was one of the great figures of the civil rights movement. In preparing to write this book, I read biographies of him. I learned that as a child he was determined to use "big words." I reread his autobiography, speeches, sermons, and articles. I found his "big words." They are simple and direct, yet profound and poetic. His words continue to inspire me today.

—Doreen Rappaport

ILLUSTRATOR'S NOTE

When I close my eyes and think about Dr. King's life, the main image that comes to me over and over again is that of stained-glass windows in a church. For me, the windows are metaphors in a lot of ways. In the dark, they blaze out at you like beams of light. The multicolors symbolize multi races. Stained-glass windows are also a vehicle to tell the story of Jesus. And, whether you're on the inside or the outside, windows allow you to look past where you are. I use metaphors throughout my work. The four candles in the last picture, for example, represent the four girls who were killed in the Sixteenth Street Baptist church. Their light shines on.

In illustrating the life of Dr. King, I wanted to bring a fresh spin to a story that's been told many times. In some places, the imagery had to stay true to history. In others, I tried to push to an emotional level that allows the reader to bring his or her own experience to it, without actually losing the intensity or the intention of the story. Collage is a perfect medium for this; it allows me to piece together many different things that have no relationship to each other, until they're put together to form a oneness.

—Bryan Collier

Everywhere in Martin's hometown,
he saw the signs, **WHITE ONLY**.
His mother said these signs were
in all Southern cities and towns
in the United States.
Every time Martin read the words,
he felt bad,
until he remembered what
his mother told him:

"You are as good as anyone."

In church Martin sang hymns.
He read from the Bible.
He listened to his father preach.
These words made him feel good.

"When I grow up, I'm going to get big words, too."

Martin grew up.
He became a minister like his father.
And he used the big words
he had heard as a child
from his parents and from the Bible.

"**Everyone
can be
great.**"

He studied the teachings of Mahatma Gandhi.
He learned how the Indian nation won freedom
without ever firing a gun.
Martin said "love,"
when others said "hate."

**"Hate cannot
drive out hate.
Only love
can do that."**

He said "together"
when others said "separate."
He said "peace"
when others said "war."

"Sooner
or later,
all the people
of the world
will have to
discover a way
to live together."

In 1955 on a cold December day
in Montgomery, Alabama,
Rosa Parks was coming home from work.
A white man told her to get up
from her seat on the bus so he could sit.
She said No, and was arrested.

Montgomery's black citizens learned of her arrest.
It made them angry.
They decided not to ride the buses
until they could sit anywhere they wanted.

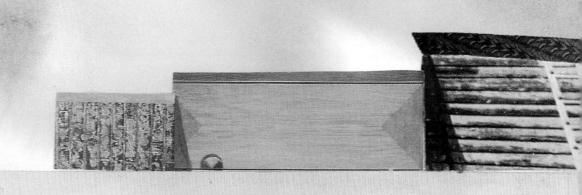

For 381 days they walked
to work and school and church.
They walked in rain and cold
and in blistering heat.
Martin walked with them and talked with them
and sang with them and prayed with them
until the white city leaders had to agree
they could sit anywhere they wanted.

"When the history
books are written,
someone will say
there lived black people
who had the courage
to stand up for
their rights."

In the next ten years, black Americans all over the South
protested for equal rights.
Martin walked with them and talked with them
and sang with them and prayed with them.

White ministers told them to stop.
Mayors and governors and police chiefs and judges
ordered them to stop.
But they kept on marching.

"Wait! For years I have heard the word 'Wait!' We have waited more than three hundred and forty years for our rights."

They were jailed
and beaten
and murdered.
But they kept on marching.
Some black Americans wanted
to fight back with their fists.
Martin convinced them not to,
by reminding them of
the power of love.

"Love is the key to the problems of the world."

Many white Southerners hated and feared
Martin's words.
A few threatened to kill him and his family.
His house was bombed.
His brother's house was bombed.
But he refused to stop.

**"Remember,
if I am stopped,
this movement
will not be stopped,
because God is
with this movement."**

The marches continued.
More and more Americans listened to Martin's words.
He shared his dreams and filled them with hope.

"**I have a dream
that one day in Alabama
little black boys and black girls
will join hands with
little white boys and white girls
as sisters and brothers.**"

After ten years of protests,
the lawmakers in Washington voted to end segregation.
The **WHITE ONLY** signs in the South came down.

Dr. Martin Luther King, Jr.,
cared about all Americans.
He cared about people
all over the world.
And people all over the world
admired him.
In 1964, he won
the Nobel Peace Prize.
He won it because he taught
others to fight with words,
not fists.

Martin went wherever people needed help.
In April 1968 he went to
Memphis, Tennessee.
He went to help garbage collectors
who were on strike.
He walked with them and talked with them
and sang with them and prayed with them.

On his second day there,
he was shot.

He died.

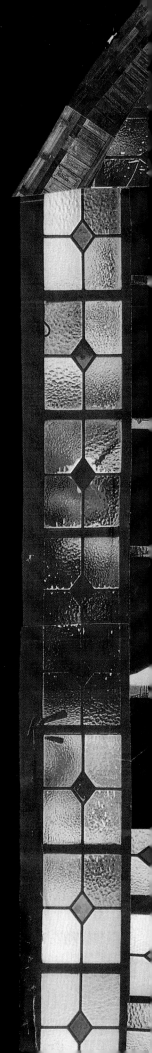

Freedom

PEACE

His big words are alive for us today.

Together

I have a dream

LOVE

Important Dates

January 15, 1929: Martin Luther King, Jr., is born in Atlanta, Georgia.

June 18, 1953: Coretta Scott and Martin Luther King, Jr., are married.

May 17, 1954: In Brown v. Topeka Board of Education, U.S. Supreme Court declares racial segregation in public schools unconstitutional.

November 17, 1955: Yolanda Denise King is born.

December 5, 1955–December 21,1956: Montgomery Bus Boycott.

January 10–11, 1957: The Southern Christian Leadership Conference is founded and Dr. King is chosen president.

October 23, 1957: Martin Luther King III is born.

February 1, 1960: The first sit-in in Greensboro, North Carolina.

January 30, 1961: Dexter Scott King is born.

November 1961–August 1962: Albany, Georgia, Protest Movement.

March 28, 1963: Bernie Albertine King is born.

April–May 1963: Birmingham, Alabama, Protest Movement.

August 28, 1963: Dr. King's "I Have a Dream" speech at the March on Washington.

January 23, 1964: The 24th Amendment eliminates the poll tax in Federal elections.

July 2, 1964: The Civil Rights Act is signed prohibiting discrimination in public accommodations and in employment.

December 10, 1964: Dr. King is awarded the Nobel Peace Prize.

January–March 1965: Selma, Alabama, Protest Movement.

August 6, 1965: The Voting Rights Act becomes law.

April 4, 1968: Dr. King is assassinated.

April 11, 1968: President Johnson signs the second Civil Rights Act.

October 19, 1981: The Martin Luther King, Jr., Center for Non-Violent Change, also called the King Center, opens in Atlanta, Georgia.

November 22, 1982: U.S. Senate approves the erection of a monument to Dr. King in Washington, D.C.

January 15, 1986: Dr. King's birthday is celebrated as a national holiday for the first time.

Additional Books and Web Sites

Adler, David A. *A Picture Book of Martin Luther King, Jr.* New York: Holiday House, 1989.

Colbert, Jan, editor. *Dear Dr. King: Letters from Today's Children to Dr. Martin Luther King, Jr.* New York: Hyperion Books, 1998.

George, Linda, and Charles George. *Civil Rights Marches.* New York: Children's Press, 1999.

King, Jr., Dr. Martin Luther, and Coretta Scott King. *I Have a Dream.* New York: Scholastic, 1963, 1997.

Levine, Ellen. *If You Lived at the Time of Martin Luther King.* New York: Scholastic, 1994.

Marzollo, Jean. *Happy Birthday, Martin Luther King.* Illustrated by Brian Pinkney. New York: Scholastic, 1992.

Medearis, Angela Shelf. *Dare to Dream—Coretta Scott King and the Civil Rights Movement.* New York: Penguin Putnam, 1994.

Parks, Rosa, and Jim Haskins, *Rosa Parks: My Story.* New York: Puffin, 1999.

Ringgold, Faith. *My Dream of Martin Luther King.* New York: Crown, 1995.

Schulke, Flip. *Martin Luther King, Jr.: A Documentary . . . Montgomery to Memphis.* New York: W.W. Norton & Company, 1976.

Schulke, Flip, and Penelope McPhee. *King Remembered.* New York: Pocket Books, 1986.

Schulke, Flip. *He Had a Dream: Martin Luther King, Jr. and the Civil Rights Movement.* New York: W.W. Norton & Company, 1995.

The cover art of *Martin's Big Words* is based on a photograph of Dr. Martin Luther King, Jr., taken by Flip Schulke. Mr. Schulke is an award-winning photojournalist with a forty-year career working for many magazines, including *Life*, *Look*, *Ebony* and *National Geographic*. He has one of the largest privately held collections of photographs of Dr. King and the civil rights movement. Many of these photographs can be viewed on his Web site, www.flipschulke.com.

To find Web sites, use the name **Martin Luther King** as your search word. There are more than two hundred Web sites focusing on Dr. King, Martin Luther King Day, and related civil rights events. www.thekingcenter.com will take you directly to the King Center in Georgia.